The Road Less Traveled

A GUIDE TO A POSITIVE MARRIAGE

LISA CASSMAN

Halo ●●●●
Publishing International

Paperback ISBN: 978-1-61244-502-1
Library of Congress Control Number: 2012916583

Printed in the United States of America

Published by Halo Publishing International
1100 NW Loop 410
Suite 700 - 176
San Antonio, Texas 78213
Toll Free 1-877-705-9647
Website: www.halopublishing.com
E-mail: contact@halopublishing.com

THE ROAD LESS TRAVELED
A GUIDE TO A POSITIVE MARRIAGE

I am writing this in hopes that more spouses can be focused on what should be represented in a marriage, and STAY focused by dating your spouse. And to remember the reason why you fell in love. I am so thankful for a marriage built on trust and respect.

PERSONAL NOTE TO MY HUSBAND, STEVE!

I would like to thank you personally for some things you have chosen to do for me. I appreciate you more then you could ever know. Our love will withstand anything. I will not take our love or you for granted! Anyone that can do the things you have done for me deserves the best...

Thank you for:

- A beautiful wedding, you gave me something that went beyond what I could ever imagine: an outside winter wedding!
- Helping me shovel snow. I have so much fun out in the snow with you!
- Caring and worrying about me during thunderstorms.
- Knowing you are hard to get mad at! I may get upset, but you are so positive, and I like how you want to talk things out and not get mad.
- Having a great sense of humor. I like how you want to have fun.
- Giving yourself to me, and making our love great and fun!

- Loving me enough to take me as your wife.
- Allowing me to eat the last bite of yummy desserts!
- Liking my family!
- Taking the time and being patient with me as I flew in an airplane for the first time.
- There are so many more... Too numerous to mention!

Thank you, Steve Cassman. You are my best friend, boyfriend and husband. Our marriage may not be perfect, but it is perfect in my eyes. There are far more positive, encouraging things you do and say than negative things. I try to focus on the positive.

Contents

INTRODUCTION

Each one of us needs to come to an understanding of who we are before we can begin to be happy in our marriages. Take the time to read your Bible and pray together daily. Your time with God is so important to seek what he has in store for you.

I have written some positive thoughts and ideas that will help each one of us to focus on a more rewarding marriage. Take the time to read and study this together as a couple. Do not use it to criticize, but to lift each other up and to remember the reason why you started dating and got married in the first place.

When God created us, what materials did He use? *Genesis 1:27*

How do you think God sees you and how do you think we were made? *Psalms 139:13-16*

Whom do you think God created you to be?

When you learn who you are, then you can become the spouse you should be.

1
PRE-MARRIAGE DATING TIPS

Be wise in whom you choose for a partner. Do not settle; no need to rush. If you jump into a relationship, you may soon regret it. It may not be easy to get out of.

HONEY-DO: Some questions to ask yourself as you are getting more serious:

- Am I happy as an individual? If you have issues from either your childhood or a past Relationship, there is a chance you will carry problems with you. It may be that you are trying to find someone to cover up the pain.
- Are you seeing any red flags? Trust yourself enough to believe in your gut reactions.
- Are there any doubts in your mind? Listen to your heart.
- Are you respected and encouraged, instead of discouraged?
- Are you being controlled? It could be something small, but end up being big!
- Do you tell yourself and others how great this relationship is, when you are really trying to convince yourself that's true?

2

PLANNING A CEREMONY

After years of performing many wedding ceremonies as an officiant, I have found a few basic, helpful hints before you get too far into planning.

HONEY-DO:
- After the date is planned, find an officiant to perform the ceremony. We get busy and may not be available for last minute bookings.
- My belief is both of you should be involved in planning. Grooms like to think it is about the bride only, but in reality, your marriage is about both of you, so plan the ceremony around both of you.
- There are many websites to look at for different ceremony ideas.
- Pick a special unity idea, one that you both will think about in the future as a reminder that you can't and won't be separated.
- It is okay to have the input of parents, but remember: this is your wedding ceremony—not your parents'!
- Have fun and don't stress out!

3

SECOND MARRIAGE

It is every girl's dream to have that perfect wedding. From Dad giving her away, to the beautiful white dress, flowers, and decorations! You can spend years or months planning it. The day comes and it is as perfect as you had planned. You plan on it lasting forever.

But not all marriages last. That fairy tale marriage has ended. It may end for many different reasons. But that doesn't mean a second marriage has to meet the same end. You can learn from the past experience to make this one work.

HONEY-DO:
- Do not compare this relationship with a prior one. Make this one unique and special in your own way.
- Consider this a "Do Over" and handle the issues and conflicts which arise in this one differently to the last one.
- Remember it is called the past for a reason. Let it go and move forward with a different attitude and a new respect for your relationship.

4

TAKE THE TIME TO COMPLIMENT ONE ANOTHER

Anytime you pay someone a compliment, it will become easier to compliment more and more. You may actually start to believe your spouse is worth something. And they will start to believe they are worth something, and that they are appreciated.

Keep dwelling on the positive and you will both start to believe in the greatness of one another. If it is the husband telling the wife she is beautiful, she will soon believe it. Also, if a wife expresses her appreciation to her husband for providing for the family, these things will make each other feel important and needed.

HONEY-DO:
- Try the following exercise. Write down a few positive things about yourself, then your spouse. Look at your spouse's answers and then yours. Compare to see how your answers correlate.

5

SAY "I LOVE YOU" AND MEAN IT!

Love is a powerful word. Remember where it comes from: God is love.

1 Corinthians 13:3 tells us: "You can do things and give things all you want, but without love, you gain nothing."

HONEY-DO:
- Take a few minutes to read verses 8-12 of 1 Cor. 13 and write down what love is.
- Love never what? Verse 8
- This is what real love is! Don't give up.

Tell Me That You Love Me
(A Poem)

Please tell me you love me.
Please tell me you care!
Don't hold your feelings back, and say,
"With you my life I will share.
Please hold me tight.
Don't ever let me go.
You need me and I need you,
more then you'll ever know."

6
ADMIT MISTAKES

It is so easy to sometimes blame others for our circumstances. Sit back and look at the situation and allow yourself to apologize and admit when you are wrong or when you have said or done something to hurt your spouse.

HONEY-DO:
- When in a disagreement, you are together in this. Nobody is a winner and nobody is a loser.
- Don't be afraid to be the one to take the first step back to unity!
- Take responsibility for your part.

7

LISTEN TO ONE ANOTHER. DONT LET YOUR MIND WANDER. DON'T PUT IT OFF UNTIL LATER...

When searching for the right vehicle, you look and look until you find the perfect one. You then take it home and take care of it, show it off, wash it and wax it. This car is your pride and joy. Until one day you decide it has too many miles, it is not shiny any more, does not run well anymore, and you want to trade it in for a new one.

Like finding the perfect car, when searching for the perfect wife, you search and search... until you find the right one. You show her off, you take care of her, and then one day you suddenly think she is not what you expected her to be. You are tired and weary, and do not know how to take care of her anymore.

This is where listening steps in. Make a concentrated effort to hear one another. Ask questions to get to know who your spouse is again, but listen to what they're telling you in less obvious ways too.

HONEY-DO:
- Ask your spouse, "Do I make you feel heard?"
- If the answer is yes, ask them what it is that you do that makes them feel the most heard.
- If the answer is no, ask them what you might do to help them feel heard.

8

BE SPONTANEOUS AND LOOK INTO YOUR SPOUSE'S EYES AND SAY, "I LOVE YOU AND YOU ARE BEAUTIFUL."

We were on a date, eating pizza, enjoying our normal time talking, when my husband took my hands, looked into my eyes, and told me how beautiful I am. The feeling that came over me is indescribable. He told me this from his heart, not because he felt he had to say anything. I thought, "When I look into your eyes, I see sunshine through mine."

Husbands, it goes a LONG way if you tell your wife she is beautiful before she even gets out of bed!

HONEY-DO:
- If we are made in God's image, what does *1 John 4:16* have to say and how does it pertain to us? How do you really see your spouse? It should be the beauty within. Make one another feel special and important.
- Read *Ephesians 4:1-6* and talk about what it means to you.

Tell Me That You Love Me
(A Poem)

Please tell me you love me.
Please tell me you care!
Don't hold your feelings back, and say,
"With you my life I will share.
Please hold me tight.
Don't ever let me go.

17

You need me and I need you,
more then you'll ever know."

9

LOVE SHOULDN'T HURT

Some ways you can hurt your spouse:
- Ignoring Them (Silent Treatment). Whether it is not talking because of something that has caused a difference between the two of you, or you decide that something else is more important than talking (without an explanation).
- Walking away and not discussing what the issue at hand is.
- Verbal attacks— Yes, words do hurt! You cannot take back what you have just said. It takes more than 10 positives to right a negative.
- Physical attacks are never okay. One spouse should not be afraid of the other.
- Sometimes a spouse will try to use sex to "apologize" for a harmful action against their spouse. The thing is, the hurt spouse is probably not feeling so intimate! This is using sexual intimacy to manipulate the relationship, instead of communicating what's going on between the two of you. This is abuse and harms the relationship.
- Lying can happen so easily when one has been hurt, to cover up for what one is feeling. Be honest with your spouse.
- Taking your relationship for granted can happen without realizing it is happening. Take time to appreciate your spouse before it is too late.
- Control can turn into abuse whether it is verbal or physical. Work together, not against one another.

- Mistrust is such a loss in a relationship. Don't mistrust, unless there is a reason to. Guard against doing anything to allow your spouse to lose their trust in you.

HONEY-DO:
- Discuss with your spouse right now where you think you stand in your relationship on all of the above points. Talk about what actions you might take to stop hurting one another in these ways, and then TAKE THAT ACTION!

10

FLIRT WITH EACH OTHER

Remember when you would flirt while dating? What was it like and how did you feel about yourself and the one you were dating?

You can add a little bit of spice to your marriage just by flirting with one another. Have fun like you used to. If you have children, don't use them as an excuse. On occasion, get a babysitter and go out for the evening. Flirt with one another! While you are at work, call or send a flirty text and spark the romance that began your relationship. This could be the start of something great.

HONEY-DO:
- At least once this week, send your spouse a flirty text. For example, "WANTED: My husband to go on a date with me tonight. He is handsome, funny and I love spending time with him. I would like him as my boyfriend and best friend! Call me as soon as possible."

11
SING A LOVE SONG

There is something about singing— whether it's along with a song or just acapella— that is amazing!

My husband sang "I Cross my Heart" by George Strait on the way to our wedding reception. It was the most beautiful sound ever. He held my hand and looked into my eyes. Ever since I could remember I have wanted someone to sing to me, and I finally have someone who does. Find out the wishes of your spouse and surprise them with what they desire. If you cannot carry a tune, remember the words and intentions mean more than the sound.

HONEY-DO:
- Think of a song which has lyrics that somehow represent your relationship or a facet of your spouse to you. Sing or play it to your spouse and tell him or her why it makes you think of them.

12

TALK TO EACH OTHER

I wrote earlier about listening; remember that talking to each other is just as important.

Sometimes we can be upset about something so we will not talk, thinking that the other person will not listen. Remember when you are talking to try to keep it positive and make sure that you are both ready for the end results to be that you come up with a solution to any issues.

You need to have your mind set to what you want to get out of your marriage. If need be, have a set time where you can have a "family meeting". You should be able to discuss things during this time that you normally would not be able to discus because of your busy schedule.

HONEY-DO:
- Set a time for a "family meeting" this week to check-in on the health of your communication as a couple.

13

LEAVE ONE ANOTHER LOVE-VOICEMAILS

If you are having a really bad day, or you are missing your spouse, there is nothing like listening to an old voicemail that could cheer you up and make your day just a little bit brighter. Especially if he/she is working or busy and you cannot get a hold of them. When you love someone, the sound of their voice can mean the world to you!

HONEY-DO:
- Make sure to save at least one or two messages to listen to whenever you want to hear your lover's voice.

14
DO NOT RAISE YOUR VOICE

If you find yourself starting to get angry, take a deep breath. All that anger will do is cause you to say things you will regret. There are words that do not need to be spoken during an argument. For example, no back slashing or bringing things up that were from long ago and should have been forgiven.

HONEY-DO:
- Read *James 3:13-16*. In the scripture, it gives us two kinds of wisdom. How can you apply this to your own marriage?
- How can you sow in peace and raise a harvest of righteousness? *James 3:17*

15

WHISPER SWEET WORDS
IN YOUR LOVER'S EARS

Whispering a simple, "I love you," in your spouse's ear can make an impact on your relationship at any given moment. Sneaking up from behind your spouse, giving them a hug and whispering soothing or seductive words can set the mood for a more romantic and satisfying day—and night!

HONEY-DO:

- At least once this week, whisper "sweet nothings" into your spouse's ear. They can be doing dishes, watching the news, or anything else, when you simply drop your line of love into their consciousness. Don't even worry if it sounds cheesy—that can make it even more delightful!

16

BE PASSIONATE

During intimacy, some couples may think it's okay to just have sex and not make it passionate and personal. After a while it may seem like a chore and you may not feel like you want to be intimate or you may withdraw from that part of your life with your partner.

If this has happened, try talking to each other about what is lacking in your relationship and try to stay positive. Try not to place blame on one another while having this conversation. Start here and from this point try going on dates, being romantic, dressing for the mood— there are so many ways you can get back on track with each other. You do not have to waste time in your marriage without intimate relations.

HONEY-DO:
- Make a point to communicate about your sex life with your spouse today. Find out what they need to bring the spark back to the bedroom. Listen to one another and take it to heart! You'll be so glad you did...

17

DO NOT USE THE WORDS "ALWAYS" OR "NEVER"

Statements starting with, "You always" or "You never" are, without exception, untrue. And they get your spouse's hackles up.

Here are some other phrases I would not recommend using in your relationship:
- Why don't you ever...
- That figures!
- Never mind!
- That time when you...
- I wish you would...
- You're just like your mother/father!
- If you love me…
- You started it!

Some phrases you may want to use in your relationship:
- I feel hurt when...
- I would like you to...
- Can we...
- I like it when...
- I appreciate...

HONEY-DO:
- Next time an argument comes up, be intentional in how you choose your words. Give the suggested phrases a try instead of the ones from the no-no list, and see how the issue at hand is diffused!

18

REMEMBER TO FORGIVE

Once you say something, you cannot take it back. When this happens, it may sometimes feel like an apology will not be successful.

If you want to live a life without regrets, learn to forgive yourself and one another. Learn from the choices you have already made and know that you can move forward with each other.

To be the partner your spouse needs you to be, look at your own self and see if there is any hurt or bitterness you may have toward anyone in your life. Let it go.

Remember: It is your choice whether you want to work on you and your marriage!

HONEY-DO:
- Read and discuss *Colossians 3:12-14* together.

19

WHEN WORKING ON A PROJECT, STOP AND...

When you are working on a project with your spouse, sometimes it can get frustrating and you might start to get on each other's nerves. When this happens, stop and look at what you have accomplished!

Take a moment to thank each other and show your appreciation for what you have done instead of focusing on the little things that did not get done. Stop to get a drink or enjoy a meal together before finishing your task at hand.

If you push yourself too much, you will start to irritate each other even more!

HONEY-DO:
- Tell one another two things that you appreciate about one another right now. Next time you're feeling irritated with one another, find two more things to be grateful about to one another.

20

DO NOT LIE

It does not matter how much you think you can get away with when you are untruthful, your lies will eventually be revealed, especially by a praying spouse.

Secrets are a form of lying. If you know something you have done could hurt your marriage and you are keeping it from your spouse, you are being dishonest.

Anything you do online or on your phone, you should give your spouse access to it. When you do this, he or she will know you are staying faithful and honest. Being honest will help your spouse to trust you always.

HONEY-DO:
- Read *Colossians 3:5-10* and discuss with your spouse what it means to your marriage.

21

MEN, OPEN DOORS FOR YOUR WIVES

Sometimes it is hard for women to allow men to open doors for them, thinking they would like to be independent and do things on their own. Ladies, remember that when a man opens your door it is not to show he is more capable or because he is controlling, but it is because he respects you as his wife, and appreciates all that you do for him.

There are so many times when my husband opens the house or car door for me, and it is such an amazing feeling knowing how much I am loved and taken care of by him. If someone else opened the door for you at a place of business or church, would you react in a positive or negative way? Remember, ladies: appreciate what your husband does!

HONEY-DO:
- Husband, make a habit this week of opening the door for your wife. It might just stick!

22

MEN, LET YOUR WIFE SIT

As we walked into a laundry facility, my husband and I noticed there were two chairs, both being occupied by other people. We walked back by the dryers and we were standing. The gentleman sitting suddenly said, "What was I thinking, if my grandma was here she would paddle me. She taught me to always let a lady sit if there weren't enough chairs."

How many of you men can actually say you have been taught that or respect a lady enough to do it?

HONEY-DO:
- Practice courtesy toward one another today, whether it be offering up your seat or going the extra mile to serve one another with joy.

23

CLEAN YOUR HOUSE TOGETHER

Have you ever been to the point where you are so frustrated with cleaning the house and you feel like you are the only one doing anything? Make cleaning fun! Each of you take jobs you don't mind doing and work together without criticizing each other on how it is done. If you don't like what you are doing, take turns doing chores neither one likes to do.

HONEY-DO:
- Stop in between and have a bite to eat, and sit and chat about how your day is going and how much you have accomplished.
- Compliment and thank one another on a job well done and then figure out what chores you will have next time. You do not have to make it more complicated than it needs to be.

24

TAKE WALKS TOGETHER

My husband and I have taken our share of walks. We would walk to go get a bite to eat. He even walked with me in a cold winter storm to get me a Diet Pepsi. It's great to try to find places you have not been before and make something fun from something ordinary. Don't make it a chore; just enjoy each other's company! If you tire easily, find a fallen log or a stump to sit on together and take in the beauty.

HONEY-DO:
- Anyone can go on a walk, but this week, make it a date and walk together as a couple while holding hands, talking or just enjoying the beauty and the sounds around you.

25

GO FOR A CAR RIDE TOGETHER

When was the last time you took a joyride in the car together with your spouse? I find that in a vehicle, if you stay on a positive note, you can have some of the best conversations because you don't have anything to distract you and you are stuck with one another. One important thing to remember is the car is not a place to start discussing things that will or could end in a fight or argument!

For six months, my husband and I rode and lived in a truck together. We were with one another day-in and day-out. We had to learn to deal with each other's habits. We had so much fun! Our lives changed and our love for each other grew stronger every day.

HONEY-DO:
- Discuss right now somewhere you have always wanted to travel to. Could you plan a romantic road trip getaway for an upcoming weekend?

26

LADIES, TRY FISHING

If there is one thing I absolutely dislike doing, it is fishing! However, because I love my husband so much, I have sacrificed my time and gone with him. He did most of the work when we went fishing... but I did catch a fish!

I would not hold the fish for a picture, but I do think I need to try going again, just to see where it brings me. Sometimes in life, we will not try new things because we are stuck in a comfort zone. Get away from that comfort zone and enjoy life together. Share your interests with one another!

HONEY-DO:
- Each of you pick out one thing you enjoy to do that your spouse has never done with you. Schedule a time in the coming month when you can make those things happen, only, this time, TOGETHER!

27

WEAR MATCHING CLOTHES

It sounds corny, but getting matchy-matchy can be so much fun! Whether it is just the same color or the same material, or just coordinates well. Then take that to the next level, and go out to eat or get your photos taken! There's a reason why your grandparents used to do so much of it.

We have shirts that say, "I love my wife" and, "I love my husband." These shirts are fun to wear when we go out to eat. We also have matching necklaces in which mine is the heart that says, "He who holds the key can open my heart" – and his necklace is the key! Have fun with this in a way that others can see you and your spouse connecting, and you can feel the love-light shine through you both!

HONEY-DO:
- Have a look through your closet and see what you've got on hand. Pretend you're preparing for a photoshoot and coordinate your wardrobes so you look like you belong together. That's what a couple is— two people who belong together!

28
GO TO CHURCH TOGETHER

What better place to be together then a place of worship! At church, you can spend time at the altar together and worship together. This is such a beautiful time to spend together. You are showing and teaching your children values for a lifetime, and creating a stronger bond in your marriage.

Have you ever noticed that Sunday mornings are the most stressful time of the week in some homes? Because it is the weekend and you may want to sleep in, you are more likely to start an argument since it may take longer to get ready for service. Have you ever felt like that and then went into church as if nothing happened? Well, try something different, take a moment in the car before going in, apologize, and pray with each other to set your mood to what it should be.

HONEY-DO:
- Read *Ecc. 4:9-12.* Remind yourself that it is better to have a partner, so work on loving and keeping your relationship strong by keeping Jesus first. Keep Jesus at the center of your marriage.

"The greatest gift a man can give a woman is to lead her closer to God than himself." – Unknown

29

PRAY TOGETHER

Some people have difficulty praying out loud, but this should be a natural thing in a marriage. If you can talk about other things together, you should be able to talk to God together. Try it in small steps; start with thanking him for what you have. Each time you do this, it will get easier to pray.

Make it a habit to pray before meals. It is not always the most convenient thing to do, but it is a way of teaching yourselves and your children the discipline of gratitude. When you pray, try not to make it a repetitive prayer. You do not talk to your spouse like that every day, so why would you say the very same things to God?

HONEY-DO:
- Remember, prayer is talking to God just like you would talk to your spouse. Pray for your spouse, but do not pray only what you want, but what God wants for them.
- Read *James 5:13-16*. How can this apply to your marriage?
- Take a few moments right now and pray together.

30

VOLUNTEER TOGETHER

Find something you both enjoy doing and look for a place to volunteer. Whether it is at a local church, an animal shelter, or whatever it may be, you will find it very rewarding. So many worthy causes need volunteers.

My husband and I found a local church and worked with the children's ministry. We did skits and helped with greeting when the children came in to their classrooms. It was an amazing and rewarding time. It doesn't have to be a long-term commitment; you could even just serve Christmas Dinner to the homeless this holiday season! Serving together shows you different sides of each other's hearts and could help bring your relationship to a new level.

HONEY-DO:
- Discuss what voluntary position interests the both of you.
- This week, reach out to a resource in your community that would hook you up with a cause you're interested in volunteering with.

31

HAVE YOUR PHOTOS TAKEN

Having photos taken together will preserve your memories for years to come. Not just for yourselves but for your children to see how fun a marriage can be. Snapshots are fun, but take the time to get professional pictures also. You can have fun coordinating your outfits, or you can use a theme of something you enjoy together— like having them taken on the pitcher's mound if you like baseball. Have the photographer meet you to take your photos where you had your first date. When all is said and done, make a scrapbook or collage of your photos. Even if you have not done any scrapbooking before, try it with these pictures to relive the memories.

HONEY-DO:
- Do a quick online search for a list of local photographers and get in touch with a few of them this week to start the process. A good photographer will remind you why you love your spouse in the way he/ she poses you, directs you, and what they ask about you on your shoot!

32

HUSBANDS, WALK ON THE OUTSIDE OF YOUR WIVES

When my husband first made the point to walk beside me on the outside of the sidewalk, I thought that it was strange. Later I realized he was doing it for my protection. I have also noticed he does not do this with only me; it is with any female that we are with when we walk somewhere together. A man should protect a woman and keep her safe at all times.

HONEY-DO:
- Next time you go for a walk, I challenge you, as a man and husband to walk on the outside of your wife. Make it your calling in life to be her protector.

33

TIPS FOR DISAGREEING

When a disagreement arises, it may get out of hand if not handled correctly. Here are some tips to handle it in a positive way.

- Don't criticize or belittle
- Talk
- Lower your voice
- Be empathetic
- Don't play the blame game
- Recognize what is wrong
- Apologize— don't be afraid to take the first step back
- Forgive and forget
- Give hugs
- Listen to your heart, not your emotions
- Remember that love is stronger than any disagreement!

HONEY-DO:
- Think of your last argument. Put yourself in your partner's shoes and try to feel what they felt over whatever the issue was. Reverse sides and talk to one another as if you're arguing one another's point. Then bear this in mind the next time an argument arises!

34

ACCEPT HELP FROM ONE ANOTHER

Have you ever had a hard time walking up certain steps or rocky ground? It is a lot easier if you have someone holding onto your arm. I am so amazed every time I have walked up a hill or on rocks, my wonderful husband makes sure I do not fall.

Not just on rocky ground, but also in other circumstances. For instance, I do not like going in water, and the first time I was with him in the lake, he was right there with me. He makes sure I am okay at all times.

Wives, accept the help from your husband. Don't refuse the help to show your independence. Your trust in allowing your husband to be your protector shows you care enough to have him help you. And you help your husband in all sorts of ways!

HONEY-DO:
- Practice trust right now by doing a trust-fall into your husband's arms. Make sure you're both ready before you drop!
- You might also do it the other way around, if physically possible, with the wife catching the husband in a trust-fall.

35

GO ON OUTINGS TOGETHER

Especially in the case that you have children, you may not get to go on outings by yourselves very often. We all need to take a day, whether it is to go to your favorite concert, the county or state fair, or whatever the two of you used to do while dating. Try doing it more often! And if either you or your spouse likes a certain band, get tickets. You might find that the other spouse also enjoys it!

At some point, you may have had a dream about doing something but financially you could not fulfill your goals. Try saving some money to splurge on this dream! The time has come to go on that adventure you have always wanted to do!

HONEY-DO:
- Plan an outing for some time this month that you have been meaning to do for a while now.
- Discuss your dream adventure and set the ball rolling to achieve it— whether that be opening a special saving's account, or starting the actual planning!

36

HUG WITH PASSION

How many times have you just given a quick little hug to your spouse? What if that ended up being your last hug ever? Hug your partner like it is your first and your last! Some of you may give bigger hugs to your friends than you do your spouse. Are you more excited to see your friends?

Just know that it doesn't have to end up being something sexual. This may turn some spouses away if every hug has to be sexually-oriented. Try saying how much you love each other while holding onto that hug.

Once again, remember how it was when you were dating. Carry that excitement through your marriage!

HONEY-DO:
- Next time you hug your spouse, count silently in your head to at least 10. Pour yourself into it! Think about how you want them to FEEL your love coming through your touch.

37

KISS WITH PASSION

Along the same lines as a hug, you should kiss like it's your first and last. Especially when you are leaving to go somewhere without your spouse. Take the time to show your love with hugs and kissing... you will never regret that you did this! Your life and your marriage could make a big turn-around with the affection you offer one another. You should take a moment, no matter how busy you are when your spouse walks in the door from work, to hug, kiss, and thank him/her for doing so much for your family. Show this affection with sincerity.

HONEY-DO:
- We sometimes get into a rut of just speaking words, and not necessarily following them up with action. Kiss with all the love you feel! Think about how you used to live for those kisses when you were dating, and recreate those moments
- Kiss your spouse goodbye and hello every day for the entire month. It will soon become a habit you will never want to break!

38

TAKE A NAP TOGETHER

Sometimes we will get overly tired and then we start to be crabby towards each other, saying things we may regret. If you are both able, take a short nap together, even if it is for only twenty minutes.

Taking a nap together is very refreshing and will help you get through the rest of your day. If you happen to be traveling, stop the car and just rest in there. You don't necessarily have to take the nap in your bedroom, either. You can sleep on the living room couch, or outside on a blanket. Find something different and make it fun. Try making it an adventure and while you enjoy some soft music and candlelight. There are many different ways to enjoy a refreshing afternoon nap.

HONEY-DO:
- Curl up and take a nap on the next afternoon you both have off work!

39

GO TO BED AT THE SAME TIME

Going to bed at the same time together at night is so important to me. I love cuddling with my husband and just knowing we are together. We go to bed at the same time and wake up at the same time. It is too easy for couples to get away from what is important and start losing the reality of what their marriage really is to them. One spouse may stay awake and play on the internet, allowing the late nights to lead them to finding relationships online.

Many would say this will not happen, but it just starts with a simple chat room. You may start confiding in the other person then it will happen in return. An online relationship is the same as having an affair. Protect your marriage and go to sleep with your spouse as often as your work schedules allow!

HONEY-DO:
- Every night this week, go to bed together at the same time and see how you like it.

40

DON'T BE IN A HURRY TO GET OUT OF BED

Unless you have babies or children that absolutely need your attention, it does not hurt to lie awake in bed in the morning and talk about what you will do that day, or your dreams from the night before. You do not have to do this every day, but occasionally you should try it.

Remember back to when you first got married, and what it was like when you enjoyed every moment you could get by yourselves.

HONEY-DO:
- One of you get up and make a pot of coffee or tea and bring two cups back to bed tomorrow morning. Make the most of this lazy time together. You could do your devotions, pray, or just talk as you slowly wake up to start your day.

41

EAT A BOWL OF POPCORN

Have you ever had a snack attack and did not know what to eat? I have reason to believe that popcorn is a snack that anyone could, and should, enjoy! Popcorn is very inexpensive, and quick and easy to make. Make it however you like it, with or without butter. There is nothing better than a fresh bowl of popcorn to have while you are sitting around watching a movie or just having a quiet night at home.

HONEY-DO:
- Find out your spouse's favorite, easy snack and keep it on-hand.

42

LIGHTLY STROKE EACH OTHER

Talking is such an amazing part of marriage, just having that one-on-one time. But having a soft, sensual touch will keep your senses going along with that conversation! Take the time to softly touch each other and show each other how much you care. Hugging and holding hands are great, but the soft touch is so much more romantic.

Think about the touch connection a baby has with its parents. When you marry, you still crave that touch and deserve it from the love you share.

HONEY-DO:
- While watching a movie, or having a romantic dinner, softly touch your spouse's face or the top of their hand, or if they are wearing shorts, stroke their legs. You don't have to make it sexual, just keep it romantic and loving.

43

ALLOW YOUR KISSES TO BE SOFT

Think about your first kiss and what it meant to you. I am not talking about the quick peck on the cheek, or the tongue twisting in your mouth, I am talking about the soft, sensual kisses that truly meant something to you.

As with the touch, kissing is also important, you need the romance from this, the feeling of knowing your marriage is so important— and the love that comes with it.

HONEY-DO:
- Why not try it now? Take your spouse, touch lightly on the cheeks, and lean in to kiss, soft and sensual...

44

DON'T WALK AWAY FROM A CONVERSATION

While in a conversation, whether it is a positive or a negative one, it is very important not to walk away from your spouse. Finish the conversation, and don't raise your voice. It just may start an argument and then you will start saying things you will regret. If you walk away, it will make your spouse feel as if you don't really care anyway. If you need time to calm down, take a couple of deep breaths, get a glass of water, and finish what you need to talk about. If you are one of those people that feel you need more time, calm down and ask for more time to finish the discussion later and set a time to do that. Ensure you do not just walk away.

HONEY-DO:
- Practice open communication. If you are feeling overwhelmed by the discussion you're having with your spouse, tell them so. Ask if you can revisit it and plan for when that will happen.

45

DON'T DRIVE AWAY MAD

Imagine you and your spouse getting into an argument, and one taking off mad. Most people don't think clearly while angry. Driving is dangerous; you could hurt someone else, or get yourself hurt or killed. I am a true believer in not leaving while you're upset. Especially if your spouse does not know where you are going. It is unfair to them. There should not be anything bad enough to where you have to walk out, knowing that your spouse may never be able to say he/she loves you anymore. The last words as you leave should always be, "I love you."

HONEY-DO:
- Make it a habit to always tell your spouse you love them as you walk out the door each day.
- Don't ever leave in anger without reaching some sort of resolution.

46

HAVE A ROMANTIC DINNER

Plan a meal together. Think about what you both like to eat. Do you want to dine indoors or outdoors? Would you like to sit at the table or by a lake? Maybe by a fireplace? Make a date and spend some time together. After planning your meal, go shopping together and have fun buying the ingredients you need.

When you get home, decide who does what with cooking, and cook the meal together. Make sure both of you are part of the process, and you will enjoy the meal so much more. After your dinner, ensure you are both part of the cleanup also. Get out the candles and soft music to go with it!

HONEY-DO:
- Never stop dating!
- Today, clear an evening in this month's calendar to enjoy this special meal together

47

SHARE A MEAL OR DESSERT

Have you ever gone out to eat and you both got a meal, and you are having a hard time eating all of it? Why not try finding something on the menu you will both like and sharing it. If you have a hard time deciding on a menu item, the first time have what one person likes, then switch it up next time and get what the other one likes.

Something this little can be so meaningful, knowing that you can compromise on something as little as choosing an entree. Take it to the next level, and share a dessert. Many desserts are too much for one person anyway, and after sharing a meal, you just might have room for the dessert.

HONEY-DO:
- Why don't the two of you make a dessert together at home, and then curl up and split a big piece? You can even try feeding one another for a little extra fun...

48

LET YOUR SPOUSE CRY

I am not saying this to pick on men, but so many men have been taught not to cry, so it is natural for them to not want anyone else to cry. So many times I have heard from other people, "Quit your crying." But nobody has any right to tell anyone not to cry.

When a person is told not to cry, that is when emotions start building up, and soon you will become very angry and may hold back from talking to one another. Your marriage may then become what you do not want it to be.

Sometimes people need a good cry, and men, it is okay for you to cry as well. Remember the scripture says that Jesus wept!

HONEY-DO:
- Find out the reason why your spouse is crying and talk about it. The issue may be something you can help fix.

49
GIVE A MASSAGE

If you think you would like a massage, be kind enough to give your spouse one. Or take it to the next level and treat him/her to a professional massage. This is all about the touch again. It may not be the soft, sensual touch, but it is a feel-good touch, especially after a long, hard day. Take your love and let it shine through a little hand-workout. You may not know the meaning of relaxation until you have done this.

If the massage is too much on your hands, take it a step at time, starting with their feet one day, and their legs the next, etc. The feet is the best place to massage, as it takes the pressure off the soreness throughout the body.

So if you would like to really make your spouse feel good and help with relief from a long day, a massage is a great way to start with a feel-good, loving relationship.

HONEY-DO:
- Right now, take a few minutes and massage each other's shoulders...

50

TAKE CARE OF YOUR SPOUSE WHEN THEY ARE SICK

This message is for both the husbands and the wives. So many wives are the caretakers when others in the home get sick, but who takes care of her? I am very thankful, I do not get sick very often, but when I do not feel well, I am well taken care of by my spouse.

So many people have grown up with their moms taking care of them. That it is something we just expect. Do not take this too far and take advantage of wanting to be attended to. Some people will pretend to be worse than they are so their spouse will take care of them.

Be fair, and do what you would want done for you. Do not over-do it! You will burn your spouse out and may cause wear on your marriage. Take time to pray also. Show faith that God can heal you.

HONEY-DO:
- Discuss with each other what the care was like when you were sick as a child.
- Tell your spouse how you'd like to be taken care of when you get sick as an adult.

51

GIVE OF YOURSELF FULLY

When I say, "give of yourself fully," I mean, you must give to your spouse in every way: emotionally, physically, and sexually. At times, your marriage may be wearing you down, because one of you will have to work so hard at keeping it going. If you both give fully you won't have to work so hard to please the other.

Marriage does take work, but so many make it harder than it has to be. Sometimes you may feel like it is all over and you cannot go on, but remember TRUE LOVE is greater and does not give up!

HONEY-DO:
- Read *1 Cor. 13:8* and see what it says about love. Your marriage is a gift, keep it and do not return what was given to you.

52

WIVES, WEAR HIS CLOTHES

You may think this is silly, but let me tell you, there is something about wearing your husband's clothes that will help you feel closer to him. This is especially true if you can get his smell on it. Let that be something you think about next time you are looking for something different to wear.

And for you husbands: let her wear your clothes. You may just like the idea of her in something that you wear.

HONEY-DO:
* Go and have a look in his closet or dresser drawer. A pair of boxer shorts to lounge in? A t-shirt to sleep in? You might feel closer than ever.

53
WATCH A ROMANTIC MOVIE

I know what you are thinking; you are probably thinking that you do not like mushy movies. Come on and soften up. Go on a date or rent a romantic movie that your wife has been wanting to see.

Go one step further and make it a romantic comedy, and you should be able to handle that— and laugh your way through it. Remember that your marriage should be romantic, so there is nothing wrong with watching one. Then try watching other shows you each may like. And just a little added bonus, try cuddling through it!

HONEY-DO:
* Pick out a film for your next night in!

54

STAY AT A HOTEL

You don't need a reason to get away for the night. You could take the time to plan a getaway and help keep your romance going! Do you want to try something new? Take a vacation with just the two of you and replay your wedding vows. Or better yet, redo your vows with all new meaning and words. Remember the reason you got married in the first place. You do not need to renew them in front of others or have a pastor present. All you need is the two of you, and your love and commitment!

HONEY-DO:
- Have a quick google search for a weekend hotel deal coming up in the next few months. You can find budget options, or you can splurge! Either way, focus on giving each other a weekend "away from it all."

55

TAKE A SHOWER TOGETHER

Taking a shower together and washing each other can be very special. You can also take a bubble bath, sauna, or spend time in a hot tub. Light a candle, play some soft music.

Get your spouse a towel when they step out. Or you can take it to the next level by warming a towel in the dryer and bringing a warm towel to your spouse!

HONEY-DO:
- Take a few moments to think of something else you could do for your spouse that would make your shower together something you'll want to "rinse & repeat" again and again.

56

FIND THE FULL MOON

Some of my favorite times have been spent with my husband outside with a full moon. The full moon can be so romantic. We will stand outside, hold each other, and just soak in the love we share. We have had so many special memories. We have gone down by the lake, on the deck, going for a walk, and driving in the truck. The moon is what you make of it. Get out your favorite warm drink, sit on a blanket with soft music, and get yourself cuddling out in the moonlight!

HONEY-DO:
- Check when the next full moon will be, and pencil it in on your calendar. You don't need to take very long. Just get out there, hand-in-hand, and soak it up for a few minutes the next time it comes around!

57

MAKE YOUR SPOUSE YOUR BEST FRIEND

What should a marriage be? There are three things I feel you should have in your marriage:

- Be best friends. So many times we will hear someone say they have a best friend, but it's not their spouse. Your spouse is the one you should be able to talk to and share your dreams and goals with in life.
- Be your spouse's girlfriend/boyfriend. Go on dates! It's so important that you do this or you may lose the drive you once had for each other.
- Be lovers. Do not make this just about sex. Be romantic and intimate as well. Spend time cuddling and holding hands. Be passionate and make it special.

HONEY-DO:

- Check in with each other and discuss whether you feel like best friends, boyfriend/girlfriend, and lovers. If not, discuss why that is.

58

LOVE UNCONDITIONALLY

Remember that God loves us unconditionally, and we are to be like Christ. He loves us even with our faults. Love should be the same in our marriage. Which of you is perfect? We all have faults and are forgiven over and over. God loves us with all the choices we make, even if he does not like what we decide.

HONEY-DO:
- Read *Ephesians 5:25* and talk about how this can relate to your marriage.

59
HOLD HANDS IN PUBLIC

Are you ashamed of your spouse? Then why wouldn't you hold hands outside of your home? I'll bet that when you were dating, you held hands with each other. Sometimes couples take their marriage for granted, and the spark that you had— and the desire to show affection in public or at home— will go away. Start small and try going for a walk while holding hands. Don't you want to be one of those couples that hold hands still when you are retired and can barely walk?

Let others see the love you share with one another and this display of affection may just help someone else save their marriage!

HONEY-DO:
- Next time you're out and about, going grocery-shopping, or walking into church, or meeting friends for dinner, hold hands from the car until you enter the building, and/or beyond!

60

GET DRESSED UP FOR A DATE

You can go on a date anytime dressed in jeans and a t-shirt,
but have you dressed up or had your hair done to go on a date?
You may want to go to a nice place to do this. I absolutely love
dressing up for dates. It makes me feel good and gives me a
chance to woo my spouse. Has he mentioned to you that he
loves you in a certain color, or a certain dress? Wear that one.
Has she told you her favorite tie that you own? Put it on!

Honey-do:
- Think of some places near you that you'd like to go to
  on a date where you could make a point of dressing up.

61

RELAX BY A FIREPLACE

If you don't have a fireplace, find a hotel or a cabin that has one and stay there. This could be your romantic weekend getaway. Laying by a fireplace with soft music playing is beautiful. Use this time to do some talking or deciding on what you really want to do with your future together.

You could also take a short nap. Get refreshed and enjoy each other's company. The time you can spend doing this will be rewarding and rejuvenating.

Honey-Do:
- Look into a place you can stay with a fireplace, or prepare a nice, cushiony "in-home vacation" in front of your own!

62

TAKE A WALK ON THE BEACH

Grab a towel or blanket and go to the beach. Act like silly teenagers and write your names in the sand with a heart around it. Walk barefoot, squish your toes in the sand, and walk along the edge of the water. If you get wet, so what? Have fun with it! If at all possible, go to the ocean and walk in the water with the waves hitting at you. Anytime you can act silly and have fun at a very low cost, do it! You may find a side of you that you didn't know existed before.

HONEY-DO:
- Talk about your favorite beaches and figure out which one you'd like to visit together next!

63
LAY OUT IN THE SUN TOGETHER

Again, it could be on the beach, or in your back yard. Wherever it is, you could have a little rest and relaxation in the summer sun. Grab a blanket, a cold beverage, and a book, and enjoy spending lazy time together!

HONEY-DO:
- Apply one another's sun screen or tanning oil with a soft touch and a kiss or two!

64

TRY NEW THINGS

Don't be afraid to surprise your spouse with something you do not normally do. If cooking is not something you usually do, take the time to make a meal when he or she is not expecting it. If you do not usually do a certain chore, and your spouse does not like to do that chore, do it for them. Grab your spouse for a fun, last-minute excursion once in a while. Be unpredictable and have fun together!

HONEY-DO:
- Think of something you might do to surprise your spouse this week, or go ahead and act on a spontaneous idea as it pops into your head!

65

CHANGE YOUR RINGTONE TO A LOVE SONG

I love to call my husband. He has a love song for me to listen to as the phone rings. He will change it quite often or has a variety of them each time I call.

Your ringtone could even be specialized so when your spouse calls you, a love song will play. There are so many beautiful songs out there. Take the time to listen to a variety of them and choose one that suits your love story the best.

HONEY-DO:
- Set up your new love song ringtone! Or you can choose one for each other and program it on your phones to surprise one another with what you've chosen.

66

SEND EACH OTHER SPECIAL SONGS

When we were first dating, I would get emails and messages from Steve with some very beautiful songs. The words were amazing and beyond what I imagined any love could ever feel like. So many brought tears to my eyes because I did not know someone could love me like that.

HONEY-DO:
- Track down the lyrics to a beautiful love song and send it to your spouse. You could send it all at once, or maybe just a stanza at a time throughout the week.

67

BE IN LOVE WITH YOUR SPOUSE

In order for your marriage to succeed, you must be IN love with your spouse, not just love them. There comes a time in everyone's life that they must make a decision, not knowing what may come from it. I am so happy my husband took a chance with me. I thank God he brought us together.

We have both made choices in the past that could have scared us from making the choice to love one another. But the love and trust we have would not have stood a chance apart from one another. We belong together and that is something in which I will be forever grateful. I thank him for giving himself to me. I am so honored to be his wife.

HONEY-DO:
- Sit down and journal for a moment to reflect on your love story with your spouse. Remind yourself why you fell in love with that person, and commit yourself to being in love with them from here on out!

68

DON'T BE ASHAMED TO MAKE YOUR LOVE KNOWN

Whether it is showing your affection in person, or sharing it on Facebook, or any other social network, do not be embarrassed to let others know that you are in love with your spouse. It can mean a lot to your spouse to see you publicly profess your love and devotion. It makes them feel special.

You said your vows in front of witnesses; now act like it around others.

HONEY-DO:
- Get online today and tell the world how much you love your spouse. Give examples of what it is about them that you love.

Like Who Your Spouse Is
(A Poem)

And like what they represent...
Thank you for being you,
Please don't ever change,
Your thoughtfulness is known
In everything you do.
Everyone has their faults,
I know you do too.
I just seem to find
The best in everything you do.
I won't take you for granted

LISA CASSMAN

I like you for "who you are".
I've taken time to know you,
  And it's you I like so far.

69

WRITE LOVE NOTES

There are many ways to send a love note these days. You can slip a note in your spouse's lunch bag. You could also send a sweet, little text message. You can always send an email, or a message or comment through Facebook or Twitter, or any other social media. You may have fun going out to buy a card that says how you feel and then sending it through the mail, or maybe even leave a note under the pillow!

HONEY-DO:
- Use one of these suggestions or come up with your own and send your spouse a love note today.

70

WRITE A POEM

You don't have to be Shakespeare to put a few lines together that speak of what your spouse means to you.

Life
(A Poem)
Life would have been much easier
if I could have stopped myself.
I didn't mean to love you, it wasn't in my plan.
I had tried love once or twice before
and now things got out of hand.
So when you came along, I thought this may be fun.
I didn't want to fall in love with you or anyone!
I feel I have been tricked, you have caught me unaware
By being so kind and wonderful, and always being there.
It's really kind of fun, the things you say and do!
Thanks for your kind heart, and letting me be part of you!

HONEY-DO:
- Write your own poem for your spouse, even if it's only a few lines. It will touch their heart to receive!

71

TAKE ALL OF YOUR WEDDING VOWS SERIOUSLY

Just as God has given the ten commandments for a reason, you have been given wedding vows for a reason. Remember when you said your vows and in front of witnesses?

I have truly taken mine seriously. My love is so strong, because when I married, I knew this was for life, forever and always. I only wish everyone could share what we have. Please do not take your vows for granted. Once you do, you are pretty much looking for trouble in what could have been a great marriage.

If you have done anything to mess up your vows, find a way to make it right. If you are the hurt one, find a way to forgive and work on this. Remember, true love does not fail!

HONEY-DO:
- Look back at the words of your wedding vows. Think about the enormity of what you promised and recommit yourself again to loving your spouse in all the ways you vowed to.

72
REMEMBER TO KEEP DATING

I believe there are four parts to a marriage:

1. Courting, romance. You can't wait to see one another when you are apart, and then you realize that this is the person you will marry.
2. Awakening, reality. Oh no! What did I get myself into? You have just realized you made a choice, and are wondering if is the right choice.
3. Responsibility. Now what can I do to fix this and make it work? Where do I go from here?
4. We are back to dating again. Can you return to that?

HONEY-DO:
- Discuss where you think you fall on this scale of four parts. Talk about how it feels to be there.

73

RESPECT YOUR LAST NAME

Wives, when you get married, you take on a new last name. You should respect that and be proud to share what your husband gave to you.

Husbands, you need to remember that the only thing you should want to change about your wife is her last name. The day I wed, I was very honored and proud to take my husband's name. Because I love my husband so much and he has given so much love to me, I will forever be grateful that I can share his name. Remember, the Bible says we become one when we marry.

HONEY-DO:
- Remember as a teenager, writing out your name in your notebook with the last name of your crush? Do it now, with the last name you gained on your wedding day. Don't forget to scribble in some hearts and doodles. Celebrate your married name!

74
WEAR YOUR WEDDING RINGS

A ring is a circle that shows that your love shall not end. Take this seriously.

If you have a hard time wearing your ring on your finger, find another way to wear it— like on a chain around your neck. Perhaps you could have it tattooed on your finger; then you know it cannot be removed.

Some people may want to take the ring off around other people when they don't want to show they are married. Don't be that person!

HONEY-DO:
- Wife, ask your husband about his process for choosing the ring he gave you.
- Husband, ask your wife what she likes about the ring you gave her.

75

BE POSITIVE

Try to stay positive through your communication and keep on encouraging one another. Don't let the little things get to you. Keep on finding the good in your spouse and you will find that your marriage can withstand a whole lot more. Remember that for every negative word spoken, there are many more positives needed to make up for what you have said. Take a moment to think before you speak.

HONEY-DO:
- Take a few moments to write a list of positive things about your spouse. Each day when you see something you like, thank your spouse for what he or she does.
- Read *Psalm 103:8-10* and explain in your own words what it means.

76

DON'T BLAME EACH OTHER

My husband and I have very open communication and we know how to talk well with each other. We do not blame each other for the silly things that happen. We also do not hold grudges. Keep in mind that it may start with little things such as conversation that goes something like:
"What's wrong?"
"Nothing."
"Really? Is that why you are giving me the silent treatment?"

If you ask what is wrong, expect the worst, whether you like it or not. Remember with the silent treatment-- ACTIONS SPEAK LOUDER THEN WORDS! This can then lead to anger and holding grudges. The tongue is a weapon of its own. When you do get hurt, you should be able to forgive your spouse. You hurt God day after day, and he forgives you each time you hurt him.

HONEY-DO:
- Stop and pray, asking God if there is anything you are currently holding against your spouse. As He brings them to mind, ask for the grace to let them go and forgive.
- Speak to your spouse about what God is doing in you regarding what you have been holding against them.

77

CALL WHEN YOU ARE OUT OF TOWN

There is absolutely nothing worse than trying to get a hold of your spouse when they are out of town and there is no answer. Keep in close contact with each other, and keep them informed on your whereabouts.

I am so thankful that my husband, being a truck driver, has always kept me informed where he is at all times. He calls to tell me where he is for the night and where he is going to bring loads. Even if is just for one night, keep in mind that you are missed at home and you should call to let your spouse know you are okay.

HONEY-DO:
- Talk to your spouse about how it makes you feel when you go long spurts without hearing from them.
- Create a plan of action so that when you're apart you have certain expectations for communication that you are both able to meet.

78
DON'T BREAK TRUST

Once the trust in your relationship is gone, it is one of the hardest things to get back. Keep this in mind always.

HONEY-DO:
- Think of some ways in which you could lose trust with your spouse.
- How can you guard against that happening?

79

BE FAITHFUL

Truthfully, even having a cup of coffee with someone of the opposite sex can mess up your marriage. This is how an affair can start. Having friends online, chatting, or texting can begin an explicit relationship without even realizing what is happening. When another man starts listening to a woman and gives her his full attention, she can so easily fall for him without fully realizing it. And visa-versa.

Husbands, be careful about leading a woman on, it is so easy for them to believe you are wanting more. Wives, do not flirt with someone else or go to the opposite sex for emotional support.

Men, it is a choice— not a "man thing"— when you look at another woman. Scripture says it is like having an affair even if you look at women wrong. You both should know that being selfish is wrong. Unless it is in regards to sharing your spouse with someone of the opposite sex. In that case, be as selfish as you can be and DON'T SHARE!

HONEY-DO:
- We all know couples who have fallen apart due to marital unfaithfulness. Talk with your spouse about one of these friends. Talk about how it started, how innocent it may have seemed at first. Talk about how you can safe-guard your own marriage together.

80

YOU ARE BOTH ADULTS

It is sometimes easy to treat your spouse like you treat your children, but it is not fair to do this to them. We are adults and we need to treat our spouse like an adult. Once you start treating your spouse like your children, you will start losing their trust and respect.

Whatever you do, do not turn your children against your spouse. They will eventually lose respect for you, and that has to be earned again like the trust.

HONEY-DO:
- Have an honest talk. Are there times when you feel like your spouse belittles you and treats you like a child? Tell them so, and ask them to avoid the ways they do so in future.

81
RESPECT

Respect. Enough said! Respecting someone is treating them with kindness, and not taking them for granted. If you cannot treat your spouse with respect, you should take a look at yourself and see what issues you may have. Even if it is just in a joking manner, you should not ask your spouse for a divorce. It hurts deeply, and that word should not be part of your vocabulary.

HONEY-DO:
- Take turns looking your spouse in the eyes and asking them how you can make them feel more respected.
- Put into practice what they tell you!

82

SUPPORT EACH OTHER

It is important to support each other in decisions and in everyday living. Keep your ears open to what the other person wants. Support the dreams and wishes of your spouse, if it is at all possible and works with your finances and lifestyle.

Life With You
(A Poem)

You have given me so much;
you gave me your hands to hold my tears,
just when I thought there was no place for them to go!
You gave me your ears to listen,
So I wouldn't fall apart.
You gave me your mouth for the soft-spoken words
to let me know I would be okay.
But most of all you gave to me,
your heart to share with me when I thought I couldn't any
more.
Mine was shattered, but now on the mend.
Thanks for sharing your life with me!
I love you!

HONEY-DO:
- Check in with yourself. Do you know what your spouse's dearest dreams are?
- Check in with your spouse. Find out if what you think is truly what's going on under your spouse's surface.

83

GOD IS FIRST

So many wonder why their marriages and lives fall apart. Maybe it is because God is not at the center of the marriage. So often, we want things to go our way, but why not try God's way? We may be afraid we will not have things our way, and God's way may be just a little different!

So try this: take a moment to pray and ask God to be in control of your life and marriage. Do not let go of the most beautiful thing ever. God wants you to have a beautiful marriage! I once heard God quoted to have said, "Nice wedding, now invite me to your marriage" (author unknown).

After you put God first, then make your spouse a priority. Do not let your selfish pride get in the way of your marriage. Take the time to talk to God and let your light shine in your marriage.

HONEY-DO:
- Pray a prayer asking God to be your priority together as a couple.
- Brainstorm ways you might enact that.

84

YOU SHOULD FEEL SAFE

You should feel safe around your spouse, without them putting you down for your fears. There is no need to be controlled by them or for you to be controlling of your spouse. Find out your spouse's fears and work on making them feel safe and protected!

I am scared of thunderstorms, so quite often when he's not around, my husband will call me to make sure I am doing alright.

HONEY-D0:
- Do you know your spouse's fears. How can you ease them? Next time you have the chance, do so.

85

ENCOURAGE ONE ANOTHER

Encourage one another, and do not be over-critical of your spouse. It is like us to find the bad and not the good in each other. The more you complain to your spouse that they are not spending time with you, and then finding faults with what they have done, you will see less and less of them.

If for some reason your spouse is not great at housekeeping, you will find faults with that. When a spouse feels criticized for every little thing, eventually they will start finding activities outside the home. They may keep themselves busy with friends, volunteer work, or other things. If you cannot appreciate the little things your spouse does, you will see them less and less as they try to find things to do and people to do them with that don't criticize them.

HONEY-DO:
- Ask your spouse what they feel most criticized by you about in your life together. Have an honest and kind discussion about it. In future, look for ways to reframe your criticism, and build them up instead of tearing them down.

86

KEEP A SENSE OF HUMOR

I am not sure what your marriage is like, but I am telling you, mine is fun. If you can dish it out, you better be able to take it! I have a husband who is always joking. If I were to take him seriously all the time, our marriage would have been in trouble long ago.

What keeps it fun is that he also keeps things positive. I could count on my hands the number of times he has put me down. In fact, no, I couldn't, because he has not. He can also light up my day when I am having a bad one. Make your marriage fun and keep yourselves laughing. Laugh with each other, not at each other. There is a time to be serious and a time to laugh. We have so much to be thankful for in our marriage. God has given us the ability to have fun.

HONEY-DO:
- What could you infuse into your day today to make your marriage a little more fun? Try it!

87
APPRECIATE

Sometimes when things start getting tough for us, we blame others for what is happening in our lives, and our spouse is an easy target. It's also easy to blame our job, our coworkers, or even our childhood. But in reality, look in the mirror and ask yourself, "How can I change my life to make things better for myself?"

Find some ways to appreciate who you already are, and appreciate your "other half", and what you do for one another.

HONEY-DO:
- Take the time now and write down some things you appreciate about your spouse.
- While you're at it, write down some things you appreciate about yourself!

88

KNOW STRENGTHS AND WEAKNESSES

So many couples have had many battles because of little to no knowledge of what their spouse's strengths and weaknesses are. Keep in mind it could be something little like cooking certain foods, to not being able to cook at all. It may be having a beautiful singing voice or being able to play an instrument.

There could be things out there you may not know about your spouse— possibly just the foods they like or do not like. Start finding out who your spouse is and what they are thinking about.

HONEY-DO:
- Take this time to write down things you would like your spouse to know about you that they may not already know. Even random, little likes and dislikes, or past achievements. Then share your list with them!

89

SUPPORT EMOTIONALLY AND SPIRITUALLY

If your spouse is not the one who supports you when you are down, who is? Take the time to listen to your spouse. On the same token, we do not need to wear them down by constantly complaining about our own life and other people's lives.

If one of you asks for prayer, pray together. That is the bonding that will hold you together. Stay strong and let God take control. And remember everything happens for a reason.

HONEY-DO:
- Challenge yourself this week to ask your spouse each day if there is something they're needing prayer for.
- Pray about it together, and encourage them by reminding them how you're praying about it when you're apart.
- Expect God to answer your prayers in some manner and look out for those answers with your spouse.

90

SHARE YOUR FAITH TOGETHER

As the world turns round and round,
I want everyone to know what I have found.
Satan has been defeated from my life,
Which God has created!
I have the love I never knew
God wants you to have it too.
He is at work behind closed doors.
Are you checking around
It could be your neighbors!
What were you doing when they needed you?
Tell me now,
What will you do?
They were lost and never told,
We had the chance,
Now they are left in the cold!

HONEY-DO:
- Think about your list of friends and acquaintances. Is there someone the two of you might share your testimony with sometime in the next month?
- Think about that list of friends and acquaintances again. Is there anyone that could use a bit of a boost? Maybe the two of you might consider having that friend over for a meal or just some quality time.

91

BE THANKFUL

It does not matter how small or large a task is, a simple "Thank you" will go a long way. It may be regarding your spouse working, cooking, or even taking out the trash. We have gotten so accustomed to our spouse doing little tasks that we forget to express our gratitude! We thank our family and friends for the same things, but not our spouses.

HONEY-DO:

- Write a list of five things your spouse does in your lives that you are thankful for and then make sure to thank them for it!

92

DON'T PUT YOUR SPOUSE
DOWN TO OTHERS

Sometimes when we talk to our friends, we have a tendency to speak badly about our spouses. It is okay to vent, but be careful to whom you are venting. It could be very harmful to your relationship if you say the wrong things to the wrong people.

HONEY-DO:
- *James 5:9* says not to grumble. Read this verse and apply it to your marriage. So much can be said about your character if you live by this scripture, and others see the love shine through you.
- Read *James 3:1-10* and talk about what this means to you and how how it can affect your marriage. So many people go to church, praise God, and then go home to say mean, hurtful things to their loved ones. These words, once said, cannot be taken back.

93

GIFTS CAN BE NICE

Gifts given to us are nice; however, so many people think they can buy love. You do not need to do that. You also do not need to buy expensive gifts. I am very happy with just a homemade card for a gift. I used to like the little gifts my children made in school. They were so special and meaningful. Now I am happy to get a text or phone call from them on the special days.

From my husband, I like the times we can go for a walk or do something simple. It does not have to cost a lot of money. It will make the days brighter by having a movie night or going out for a romantic dinner. I am very happy with a nice card once in a while or going somewhere special.

A few days after I wrote this page, my husband sent me the most wonderful card and treat in the mail. He is so awesome!

HONEY-DO:
- This week, go out and find your spouse a little something that you know they'd love. It need not be expensive or big and flashy, just something that made you think of them and that will warm their heart!

94

SUPPORT FAMILY FINANCIALLY

In some marriages, the wife will be the primary source of income. In most, however, the husband is the financial provider. Whoever is chosen for this role, ensure it is a role that is done willingly and that the person is not feeling they alone are burdened with this task of providing.

Do not use the fact that you are the working partner against your spouse. My husband has supported us for a long time, and I have had part-time jobs, but he very willingly supported us both while we were on the road. I am very thankful for what he has done and sacrificed for us. I know it is not easy.

Do not take your spouse's job for granted.

HONEY-DO:

- What can you do today to help ease some of the stress on the breadwinner of the family? Have a productive conversation about what they'd most like for you to do to help in this area.

95

BELIEVE IN YOUR SPOUSE

The day you wed, you became one with your spouse, reciting vows that you (hopefully) meant. As a single person, you can do whatever you want, but in marriage, you have a whole new reason to believe in another person besides yourself, to encourage them toward their dreams and to be the best person that they can be. One of my favorite things about my husband is how he encourages me to keep moving toward my goals and new dreams, rather than just stopping where I am.

HONEY-DO:
- If your spouse wants to try out a new career, and it is financially acceptable, do you feel he/she should be able to?
- If you have had a dream of a new career, and have not pursued it, take the time to take the next step and see where God will bring you. Remember to pray together and always make the decision as a couple.

96

HAVE FUN TOGETHER

So many couples take what they have and, after a few years of marriage, start to lose their spark and take each other too seriously.

I know I have not been married to my husband very long, but I do know that it is awesome when someone says something about us being so in love. There is nothing more precious than knowing that even around others, we can shine and keep the "US" alive.

As I have mentioned previously, our marriage is not perfect, but I am sure going to keep the love we have shining and not let the little things get in the way of our love for each other.

HONEY-DO:
- Sit down and discuss what your spouse has done for you and with you over the years to make you laugh and brighten your spirits. Thank them for being there for you in this way, and don't take the life you have built together for granted!

97

DON'T GO TO BED MAD

How many times have you heard this? We have been told this over and over again. You cannot just hear it; listen to it! Can you even get a good night's sleep if you do go to bed mad? Do you take it one-step further and sleep somewhere else when you are mad?

HONEY-DO:
- Read *Ephesians 4:26-27* and think about what it says. Think of some reasons why you have gotten mad before you have fallen asleep, and should you have been mad?
- Write your thoughts down here so you can remember them.

98

IF I COULD HAVE ONE WISH...

I can honestly say, if I could have a wish, it would be to have the ability to make everyone's marriage as wonderful as mine. That is the reason for writing this, to give ideas to others on what they could do differently in their marriage. I know that in ten, twenty or even fifty years from now I will be saying the same things I am now, because Steve and I understand each other and communicate well.

It may not always be easy, but neither of us will give up. Our love is centered on God, and is strong enough to take what life has to throw at us!

Keep making your spouse feel special. And remember to keep your marriage promises.

Do any of us understand why we go through trials? It does not happen always, but there are times when we may get angry when others hurt us, whether it is our spouse, family, friends or neighbors. We tend to blame God or those close to us. Yes, people may hurt you, but it is how you react that matters, and how you handle it.

We are not made to be doormats for people to walk on, so stand tall and look at yourself as a child of God. Tell yourself you are worth something and God created you to be the person he wants you to be: in His image!

HONEY-DO:
- *James 1:2-6* says, "Consider it pure joy my brothers,

when you face trials..." When you are hurt by something or someone, it is your choice to ask God to help you through it.

- *Ephesians 4:32* says to do what? Your marriage will be healthier if you let go of your past hurts!

99

FINAL HONEY-DOS...

Together, spend some time thinking through and discussing these final questions.

- If you could change one thing in your marriage to make it better, what would it be? (Try not to be negative about your spouse as you answer this...)
- What could be some outside influences that could be affecting your marriage?
- Are you running from someone or something from your past?
- Is there any one thing that seems impossible that you are hoping for?
- Is there any one person that you need to forgive?

Some verses to read and live by. Apply them to your marriage!
- ➢ Proverbs 12:18
- ➢ Proverbs 25:24
- ➢ Proverbs 19
- ➢ Proverbs 19:3
- ➢ Proverbs 21
- ➢ 1 Timothy 3:1-3
- ➢ Ephesians 5:22-23
- ➢ 1 Corinthians 7:1-6
- ➢ 1 Peter 3:1-7

Finally, take what you have observed and read in this book as experience you can take with you into your future. Keep your old memories, create some new ones, and become the couple that keeps falling in love over and over and over again!

CPSIA information can be obtained
at www.ICGtesting.com
Printed in the USA
FFOW02n1045270817
39228FF

9 781612 445021